ERTE

ERTÉ

ALL COLOUR PAPERBACK

ACADEMY EDITIONS · LONDON

ACKNOWLEDGEMENTS
   We would like to thank the Grosvenor Gallery for supplying photographs of works in their possession, and especially Mr and Mrs Eric Estorick for their invaluable help. Thanks also go to the Parkin Gallery for permission to photograph works during their exhibition of Erté drawings.

First published in Great Britain in 1978 by
Academy Editions, 7/8 Holland Street, London W8

SBN 85670 390 7

Printed and bound in Hong Kong

FOREWORD
by Erté

Sitting at my desk in the apartment where I have lived for more than 40 years, I find it difficult to add to the information contained in the many articles and books published about my life and in my memoirs *Things I Remember.*

At the risk of boring the reader, I can only repeat that my work has been the most important, satisfying and gratifying part of my life. I consider myself most privileged and fortunate at the age of 85 to be able to continue working with great enthusiasm and, may I say, inspiration. But perhaps more important than my ability to work is the never ending demand for it. I rejoice in the variety of work I am asked to do, from graphic work to designs and posters illustrating a variety of events, amongst many other projects.

All this work involves me in a great deal of travel, which although sometimes physically tiring enables me to meet a very enthusiastic public whose expression of admiration continues to astonish and delight me. I am always surprised, and enormously touched, by the delightful gifts presented to me be it in Tokyo, San Francisco, London or New York, and I cherish them all coupled with the recollection of the moment of receiving them from the charming and beautiful people responsible for these lovely memories. What is especially wonderful to me now is the extraordinary number of young people whose admiration is expressed by letters and gifts, and whose company I find utterly refreshing and stimulating, just as old friends refreshed and stimulated me in the past.

I cannot have wished for a better life than the one I have — to be able to do what I most love, that is work, and to be able to see the admiration and appreciation this work evokes in others.

This book illustrates in large part some of my theatrical designs, as well as some designs for *Harper's Bazaar.* Most of the works have not been reproduced before, and to that extent I hope they make up for my scarcity of words.

Paris, October 1977

In February 1912 Romain de Tirtoff, soon to be known as Erté, boarded the train that was to take him from his home town of St. Petersburg to the city of his dreams, Paris. He was just twenty years old. This journey marked the culmination of his prolonged and consistent rebellion against a family tradition which demanded that every male Tirtoff should make his name in the Imperial army or navy.

From an early age Erté had expressed a strong interest in ballet and drama, developing a refined taste which sought constant nourishment in the famous theatres, museums and concert halls of the highly cultural though somewhat troubled world of St. Petersburg. And as much as he loved the dance and drama, he appreciated the elegance and sense of style displayed by his fashionable mother and sister. Moreover Erté had revealed a precocious talent for art and design; in his memoirs Erté recalls that at the age of five he was already tracing figures avidly, besides drawing and designing dresses, one of which impressed his mother so much that she had it made up by her dressmaker. Despite his distinguished Tartar heritage, the young Erté had defiantly cast aside the wooden soldiers given as a present by an aunt. And while other boys played soldier, he had preferred to construct figures for imaginary ballets, using his mother's perfume bottles which he filled with coloured water and dressed in lace.

At the age of eighteen Erté was sent to study the respectable and profitable art of portraiture under one of Russia's leading painters. But Erté longed for Paris, which had remained in his memory as a magical and intricate place ever since his visit as a child to the Paris 1900 exposition.

Arriving in Paris in February 1912, Erté found a city already infatuated with the oriental and the exotic. Enthralled by Diaghilev and by the exhibitions, operas and ballets that the dancer introduced to it, Parisian society was well prepared for a young Russian emigré of Tartar origins with a taste for spectacle and the fantastic.

In December 1912 Erté finally found employment with a second rate Paris fashion house. He was dismissed after a month with the perfunctory advice that he should abandon hopes of becoming a designer. Unperturbed, he approached the famous Paul Poiret, his idol, and the liberator of smart Parisiennes from the corset and the shapely curve. Erté was employed immediately and joined a team which included such revered designers as Paul Iribe and Georges Lepape.

Erté's future was secured, not only as a fashion designer, but also in a context which satisfied his fascination with dance and drama — stage design. In 1913 Erté drew his first theatrical costumes, including an oriental dress for the magnificent Mata-Hari to be worn in a production of *Le Minaret* at the Théâtre de la Renaissance.

Inspired by the emergent styles of Cubism and Futurism that were gradually filling the Paris galleries, by his frequent visits to the *Ballets Russes* where he experienced the excitement and delight evoked by Léon Bakst's theatrical designs, and influenced by the Russian religious art and the Persian miniatures to which he had been exposed as a child, Erté developed a style of design which in its totality of conception and its remarkable detail could not fail to command a sense of wonder. Working in gouache, overlaid with gold, silver and copper metallic paints he gradually evolved a flat linear language in which the basic simplicity was complemented by an intricacy of geometrical patterning. By the 1920s his style, confident and fully developed, was firmly integrated within the decorative style of the decade. Figures recalling the serenity of Russian icons, dressed in fantastic, luxuriant costumes, were set against backgrounds of oriental detail and splendour. Above all it was the nature of Erté's involvement in fantasy, his love of masked balls and fancy dress, which enabled him near the beginning of his career to create such effective, self-contained worlds.

Meanwhile, Erté contributed fashion drawings to various magazines, including the leading Russian magazine *Damsky Mir,* and *La Gazette du Bon Ton,* which published Erté's first signed fashion drawings. In his fashion designs Erté combined his love of elegance with his obsession for the dramatic and the unreal. His altogether feminine figures, an eye or mouth often masked by some fantastic hat or fur stole, wore costumes which were remote from everyday life, conceived in a spirit of fun, or extravagance, or dream, but never practicality. Having inherited from Poiret's house a certain literary tradition, he invented narrative or dramatic situations within which to set his figures. Erté's fashion designs could sustain the imagination, but apart from the privileged few whose lives turned around the opera and the ball, they could only remain fantasy. To Erté, seldom concerned with the everyday world, this was no failing.

In 1914 the attention of Parisian society was diverted by war and Poiret's house was forced to close, ending the eighteen month collaboration between Poiret and Erté. Erté's activities as a designer must necessarily be restricted unless he could enter the American market. Late in 1915 he submitted a cover design entitled *Schéhérazade* to the American magazine *Harper's Bazaar*. The drawing displayed all the concern for design and detail, the elegant lines and the mastery of the exotic which had come to characterise Erté's style. *Harper's* were impressed. They sent Erté a cheque accompanied by a letter requesting a monthly set of drawings for publication. The collaboration between Erté and *Harper's* was to continue for twenty-two years and was to involve Erté in a wide range of artistic activities, including designs for interior decoration and for fashion accessories such as hats, jewellery, bags, shoes, gloves, parasols, muffs and fans, hair styles and head-dresses. These designs soon began to fill the pages of *Harper's Bazaar* which, as a result, developed a distinctly 'Erté' style.

With the end of war in Europe came the boom years and life more than ever became a matter of spectacle. Paris celebrated its new found freedom and prosperity at the theatre, the ball, and the *Folies-Bergère*. Erté now had the opportunity of fulfilling his desire to design for the stage. In 1919 he contributed two scenes for the *Folies-Bergère,* thereby beginning a working association which was to continue until 1930, and which led to commissions for a number of stage productions including *Scandals* of the 1920s, *The Treasures of Indo-China* at l'Alcazar de Marseille in 1922, and *Manhattan Mary* at the Majestic Theatre, New York in 1927. In 1919 Randolph Hearst commissioned Erté to work on sequences for his new film *Restless Sex*. This marked the beginning of Erté's association with Hollywood where, in 1925, he spent a year working on several films for MGM, including *The Mystic, La Bohème,* and *A Little Bit of Broadway*. Erté soon found himself at the centre of the 1920s, the age of jazz and flappers and stylish sophistication. His work involved him in the most intriguing social circles of New York, Hollywood and Paris. His name became a symbol of luxury.

The spectrum of Erté's activities was almost complete. In the following decades he continued to apply his talent for design and his inventiveness to an outstanding variety of media, including theatre, ballet, opera, film and revue, fashion, fabric, jewellery, furniture and interior design, advertising and, from 1926, book illustration.

The revival in the 1960s of Art Deco and the 20s style ensured Erté international recognition and a continued place in the forefront of design. In 1967 the Grosvenor Gallery in both New York and London held retrospectives of Erté's work which testified to the timelessness of his designs. In the same year Erté worked on a music hall set and costumes for *Flying Colours* at the Montreal international exhibition, and designed a new, vampish face for the model Twiggy. He was seventy-five years old. Ten years later he is still working.

The following selection of plates covers the period 1911 to 1975, nearly sixty-five years of dedicated design work. The emphasis on theatrical design is an attempt to bring to the forefront this aspect of Erté's work. The drawings reproduced in this book were executed in indian ink, or gouache and metallic paint.

A selection of Erté's fashion designs may be found in *Erté Fashions* also published by Academy Editions, London.

Thomas Walters

1

Loge de théâtre
1912

2

Chez Poiret
1911

3

BENDEL'S — NEW YORK
Fashion design
1915–1916

4

FEDORA
Costume for Ganna Walska
1919

5

BENDEL'S — NEW YORK
Fashion design
1917

6

Costume for Gaby Deslys
1919

7

FURS
The Otter stage set
1921

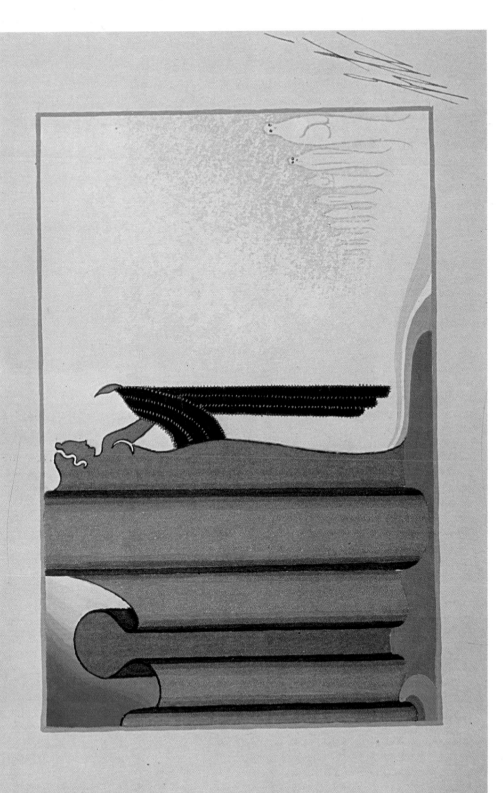

LES TRESORS DE L'INDOCHINE
Costumes for *Mother of Pearl Ballet*
1922

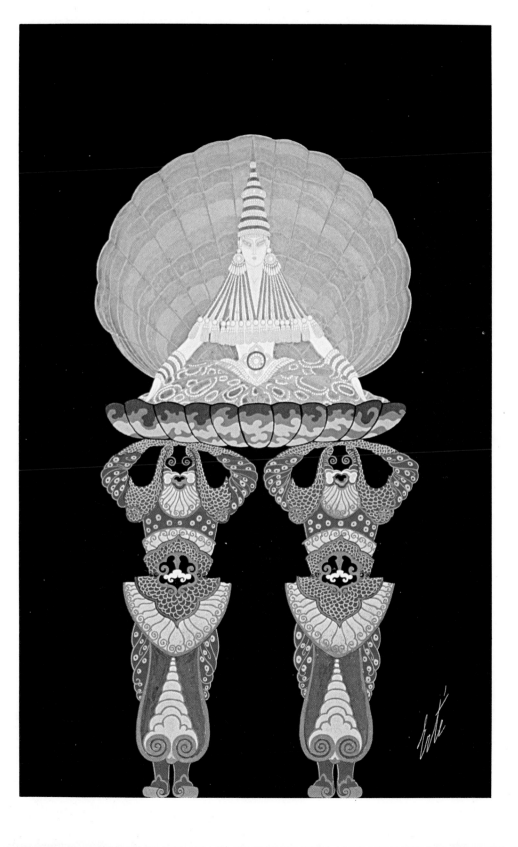

LES TRESORS DE L'INDOCHINE
Stage set and costumes
1922

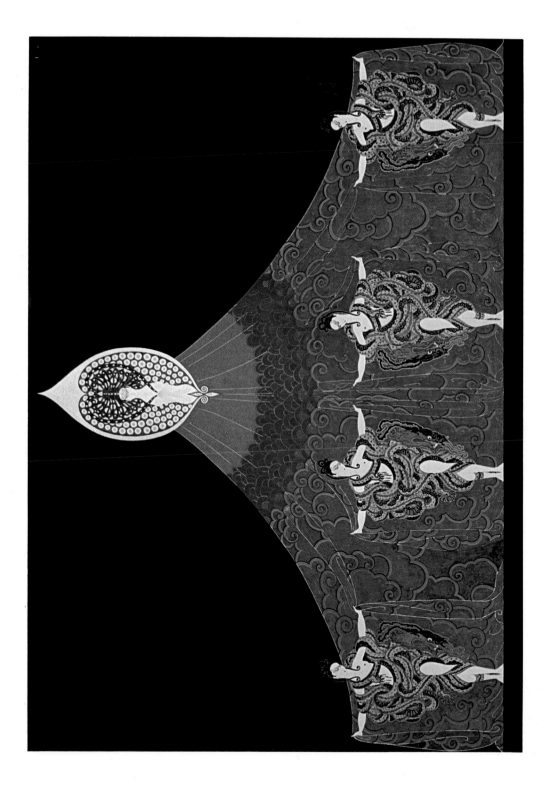

10

THE RIVERS
The Guadalquivir costume
1923

11

GEORGE WHITE'S SCANDALS
The Nile costume
1926

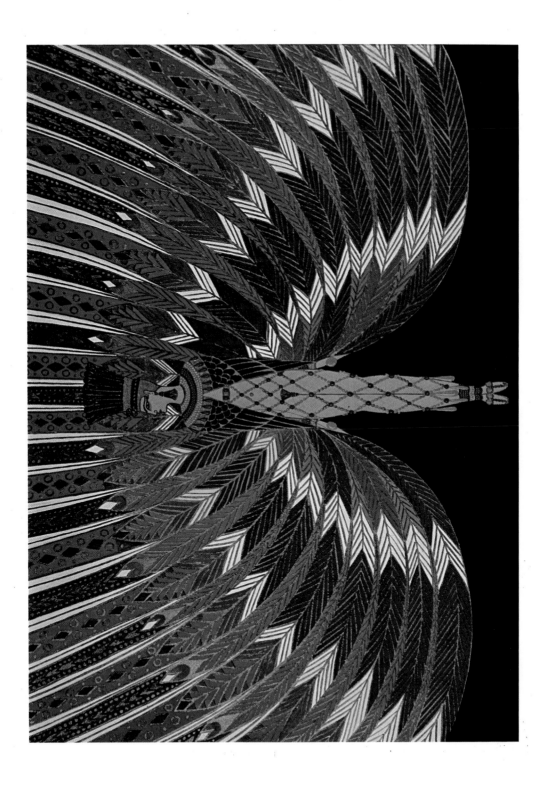

12

GEORGE WHITE'S SCANDALS
Les Papillons costume
1925

13

GEORGE WHITE'S SCANDALS
Design for a screen
1926

14

GEORGE WHITE'S SCANDALS
Angel costume
1927

15

MANHATTAN MARY
Nightclub costume
1927

16

MANHATTAN MARY
Roof Garden stage set
1927

17

MANHATTAN MARY
Stage set
1927

18

HARPER'S BAZAAR
Ombre et lumière design
1928

19

ALADIN
Wedding Costume
1928

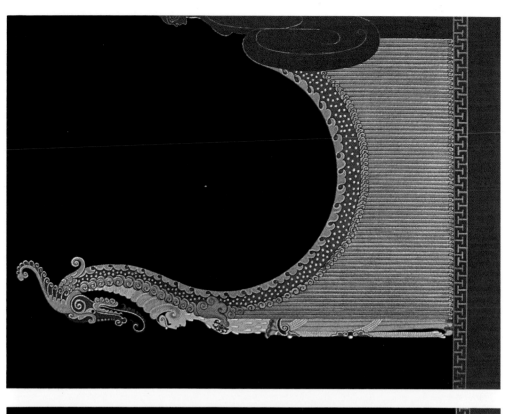

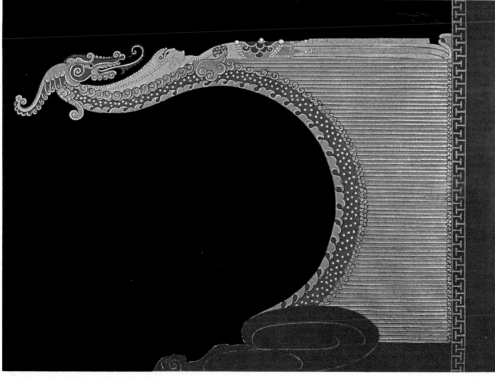

20

ALADIN
Schéhérazade stage set
1929

21

ALADIN
La Grille de porcelaine
1929

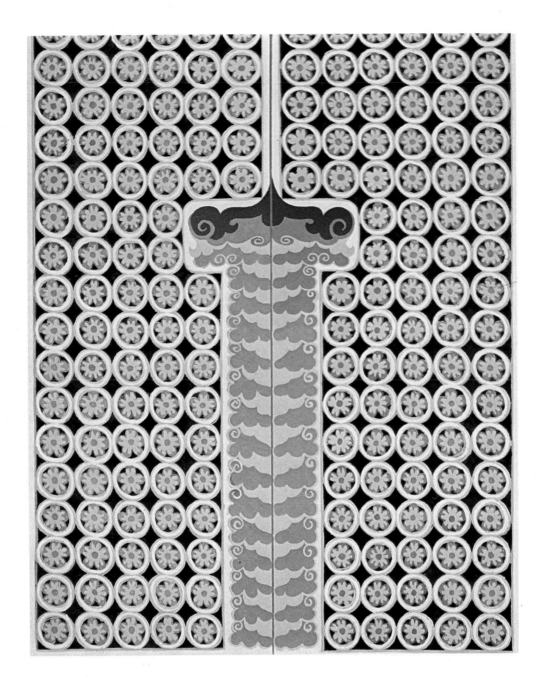

22

ALADIN
La Grille de porcelaine
1929

23

LES COCARDES
Yellow dress
1934

24

LES COCARDES
Green dress
1934

25

LES COCARDES
Stage set
1934

26

BAL TABARIN
Le Subjonctif
1935

27

BAL TABARIN
Destins
1936

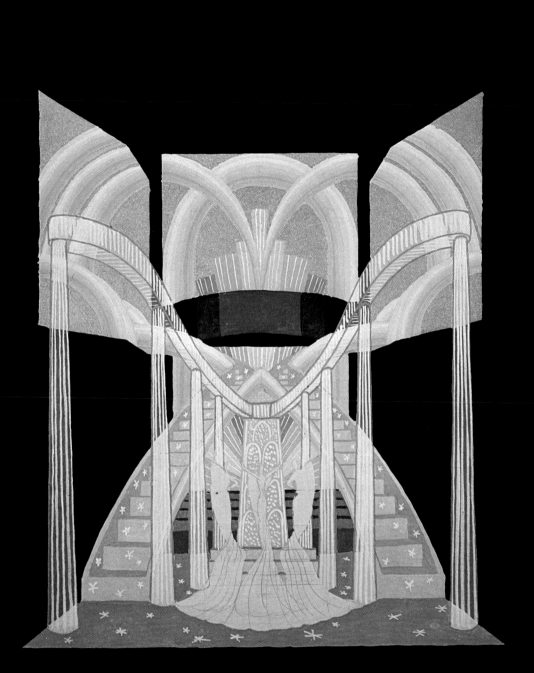

BAL TABARIN
Métaux
1936

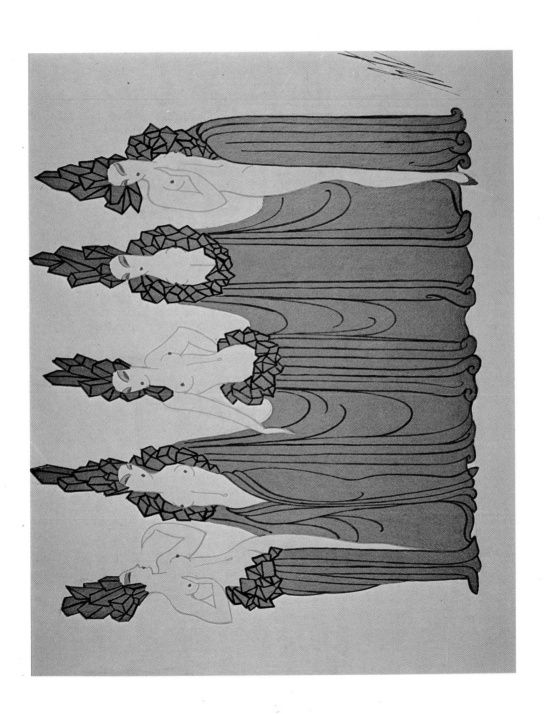

29

BAL TABARIN
Can-Can
1936

30

YANA
Design for a poster
1937

31

CARMEN
Costume for Act I
1937

32

LA TRAVIATA
Costume for Maria Kouznetsova as *Violetta*
1937

33

THE FOUNTAINS
Stage set
1938

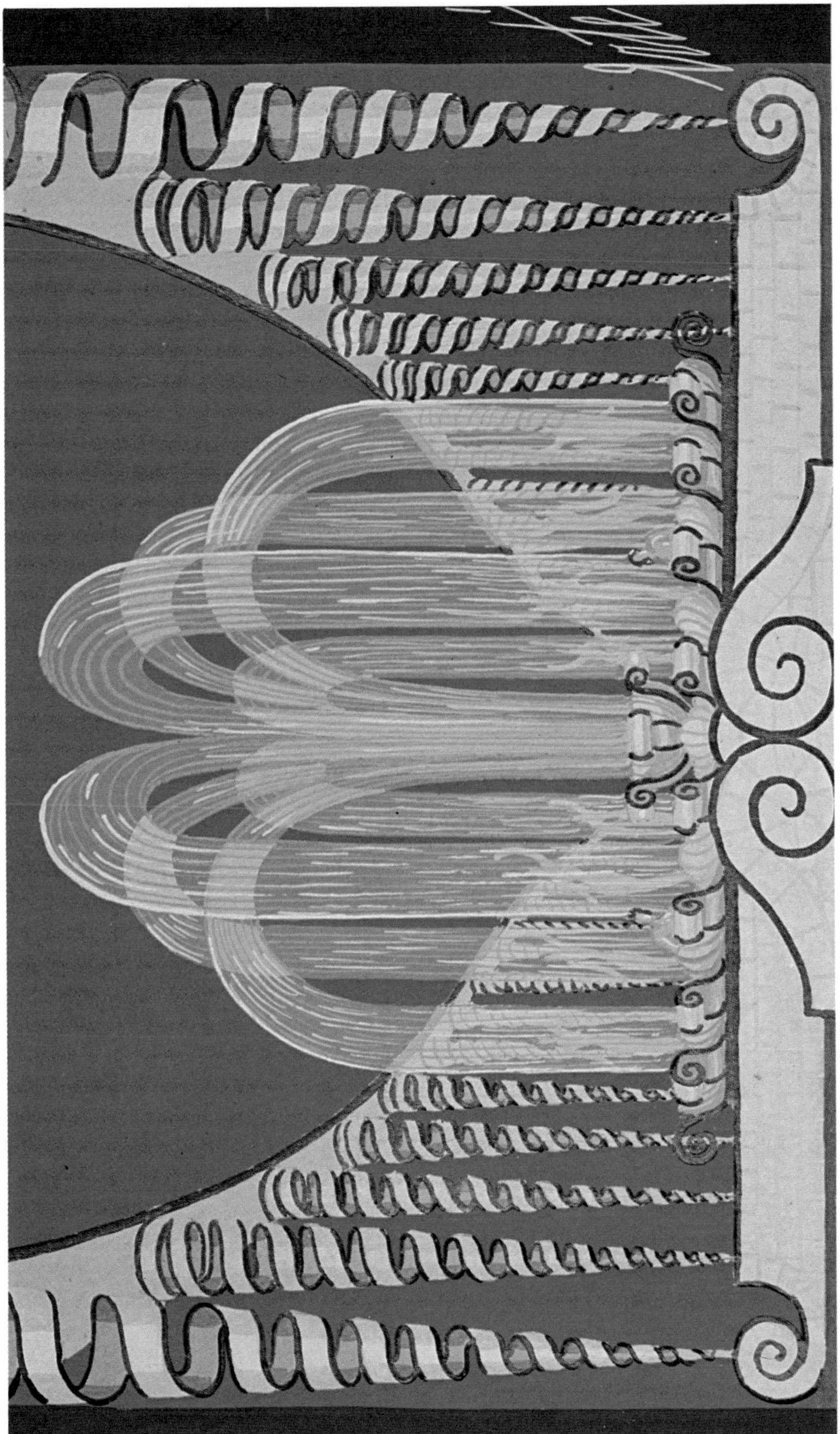

34

BAL TABARIN
Stage set
1938

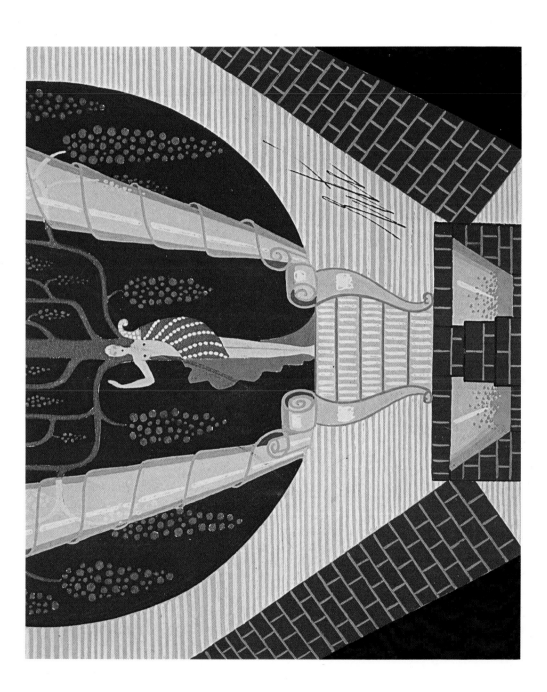

35

BAL TABARIN
Un vrai paradis stage set
1939

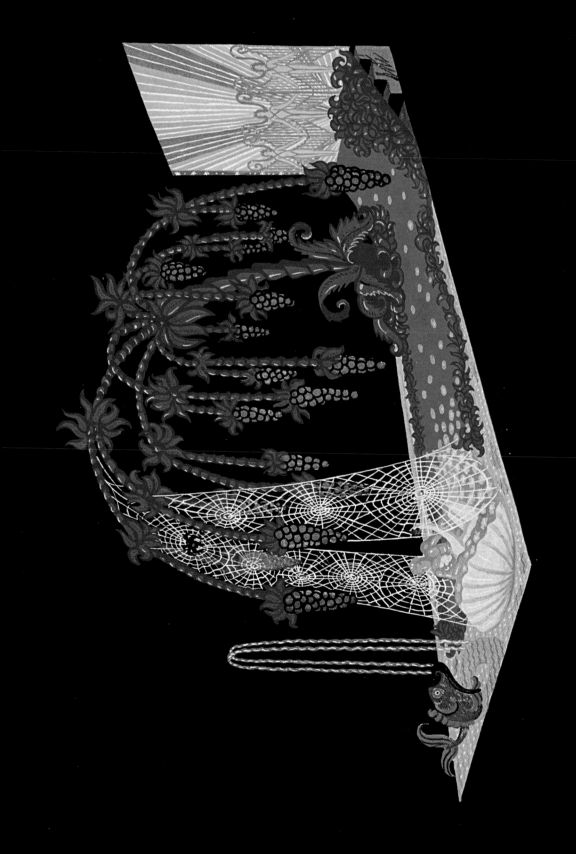

36

Second version of *Walzertraum*
1940

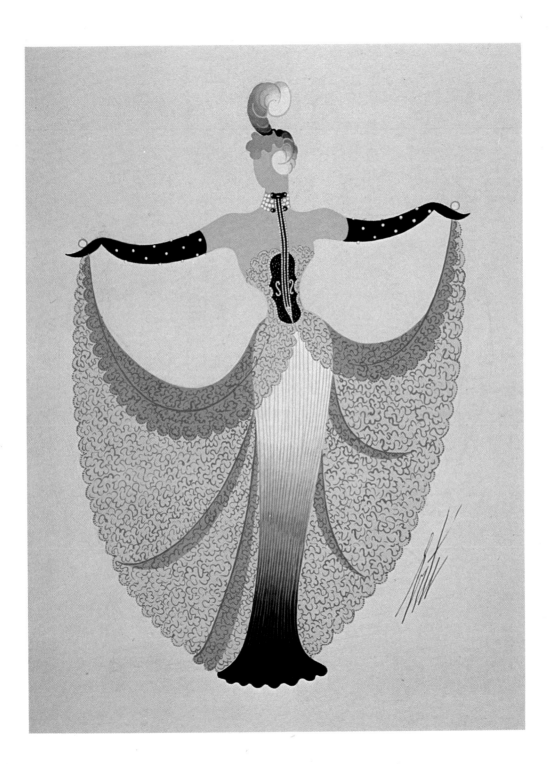

37

PHI-PHI
Costume for Madame *Phidias*
1940

38

BIRDS
Costume for *The Ibis*
1940

39

HEROINES D'OPERA
Costume for *Marguerite*
1945

40

BLONDES D'ESPAGNE
Costume
1942

41

THE RIVERS
The Guadalquivir costume
1946

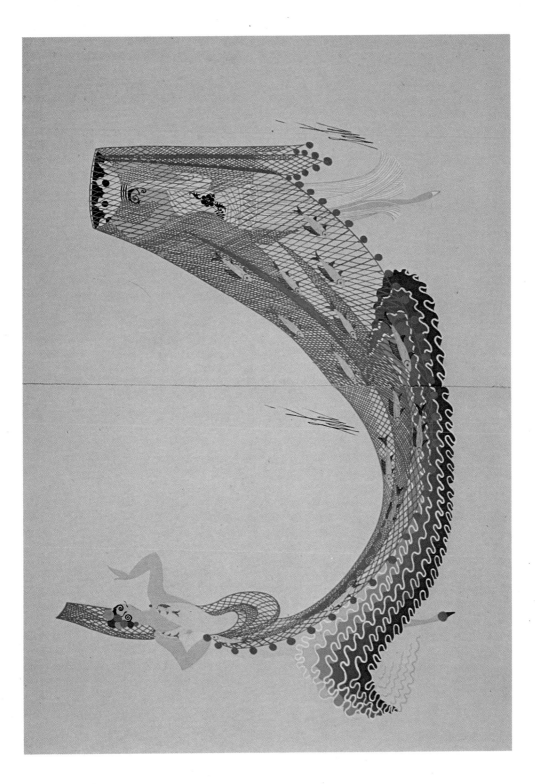

42

BAL TABARIN
Bibliothèque, costume for a young girl
1949

43

WALTZ RALSDO
Blaue Donau costume
1955

44

DIAMOND
Stage set
1963

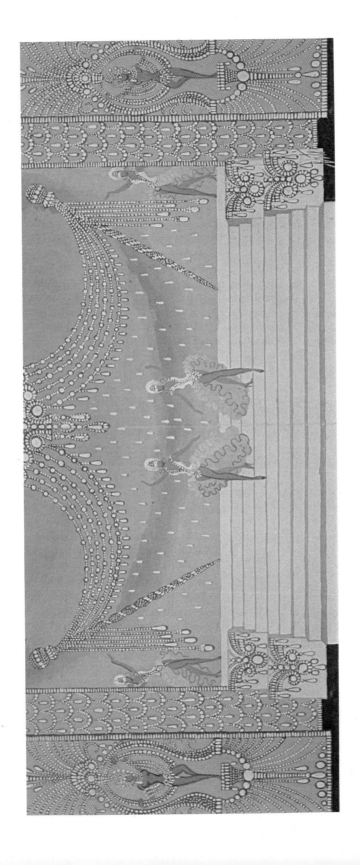

45

FLYING COLOURS
Costume
1967

46

I'VE GOT RHYTHM
Costume
1975

47

ZIZI JE T'AIME
Stage set
1972

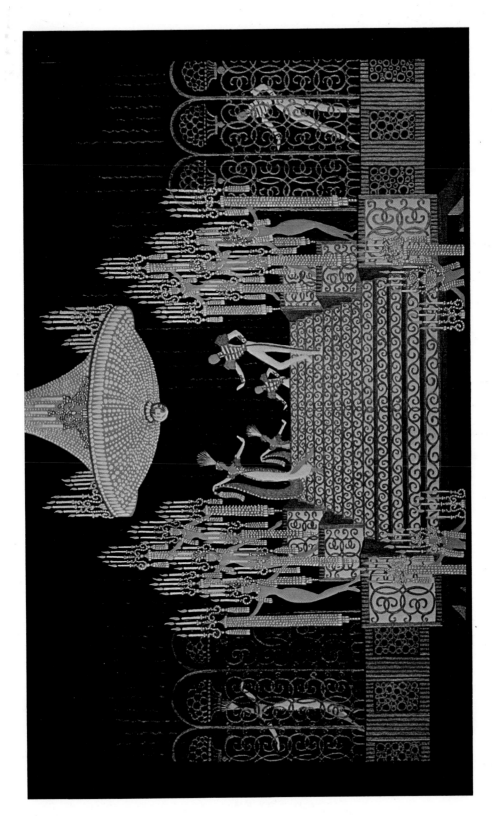

Evening dress
1975